W9-CEB-945

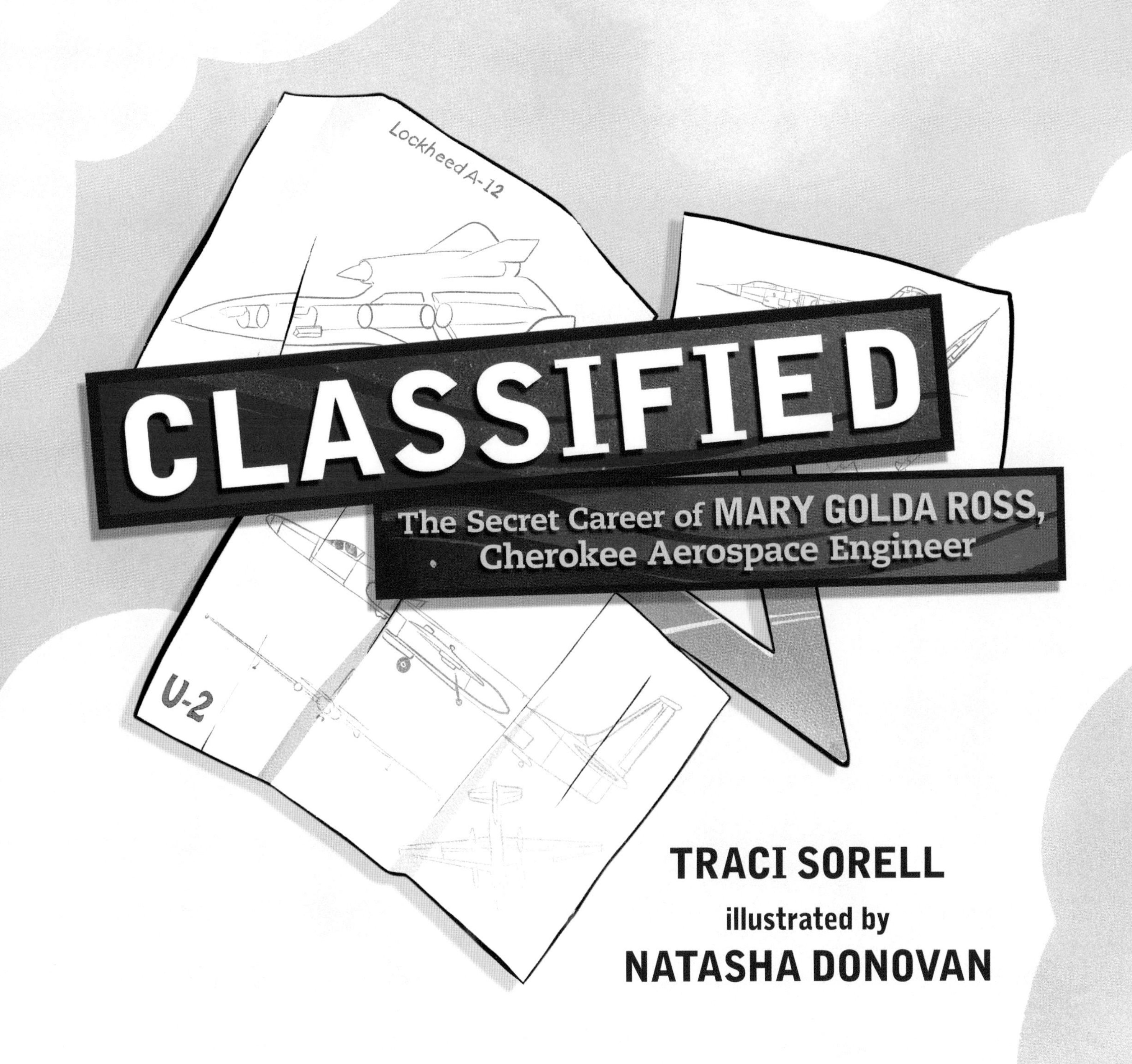

CLASSIFIED

The Secret Career of MARY GOLDA ROSS, Cherokee Aerospace Engineer

TRACI SORELL

illustrated by

NATASHA DONOVAN

MILLBROOK PRESS • Minneapolis

A NOTE ON CHEROKEE VALUES

While a written guidebook on Cherokee values does not exist, important lessons have been taught by Cherokee families to their children across the generations. Mary Golda Ross's parents instilled the tribe's values in their children. Some of the values that shaped Mary include gaining skills in all areas of life (both within and outside the classroom), working cooperatively with others, remaining humble when others recognize your talents, and helping ensure equal education and opportunity for all.

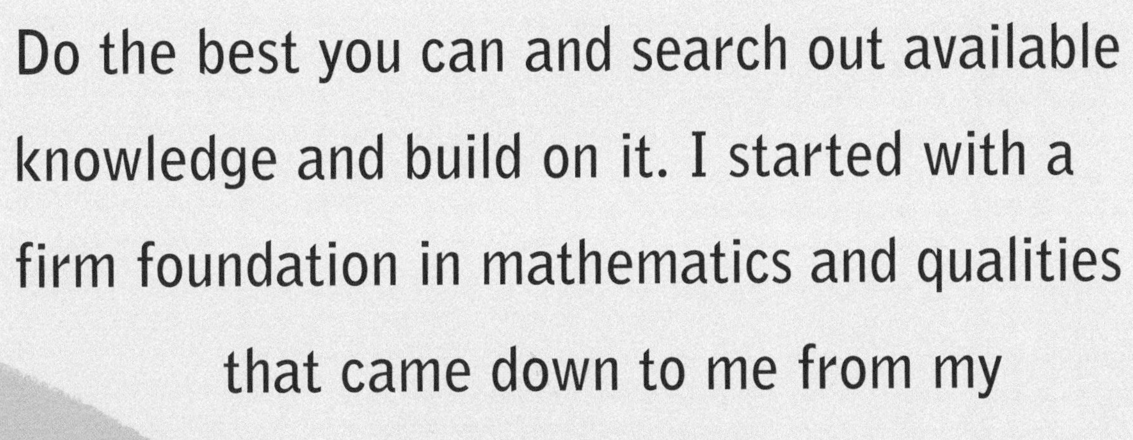

Do the best you can and search out available knowledge and build on it. I started with a firm foundation in mathematics and qualities that came down to me from my Indian heritage.

—Mary Golda Ross, April 2008

Young Mary Golda Ross pushed her pencil across the page. Puzzling out math equations made her happy. Teenage girls in the 1920s weren't expected to enjoy or excel in math or science.

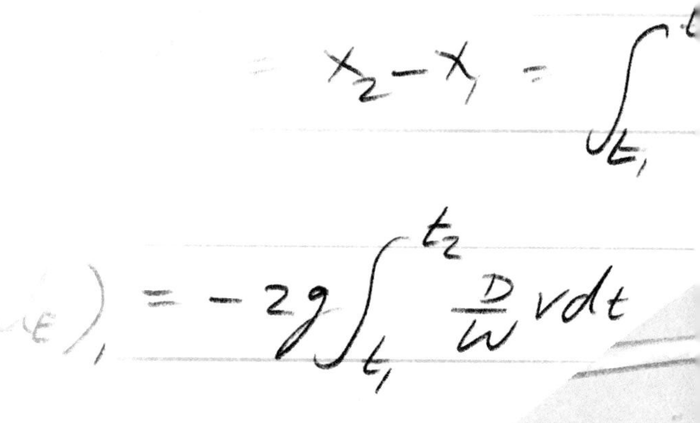

But Mary did, and she blazed a trail for others.

In the hills of northeastern Oklahoma, Mary's Cherokee tribe provided education for everyone. Her great-great grandfather, John Ross, had served as Principal Chief of the Cherokee Nation. He helped create a school that later became a state teacher's college, which Mary began attending at the age of sixteen.

When the boys refused to sit next to the only girl in math class, Mary felt motivated to get better grades than they did.

And she didn't stop there.

Holding true to her tribe's belief about gaining life skills in all areas, Mary took advantage of every opportunity to learn. In college, she majored in math, believing "the world is so technical, if you plan to work in it, a math background will let you go farther and faster."

After graduation, Mary taught math and science to high school students.

Even then, she saw more ways to grow and contribute.

Mary moved to Washington, DC, where a supervisor at the Bureau of Indian Affairs noticed her talent. She was then hired to be the girls' adviser at the bureau's coed boarding school in Santa Fe, New Mexico.

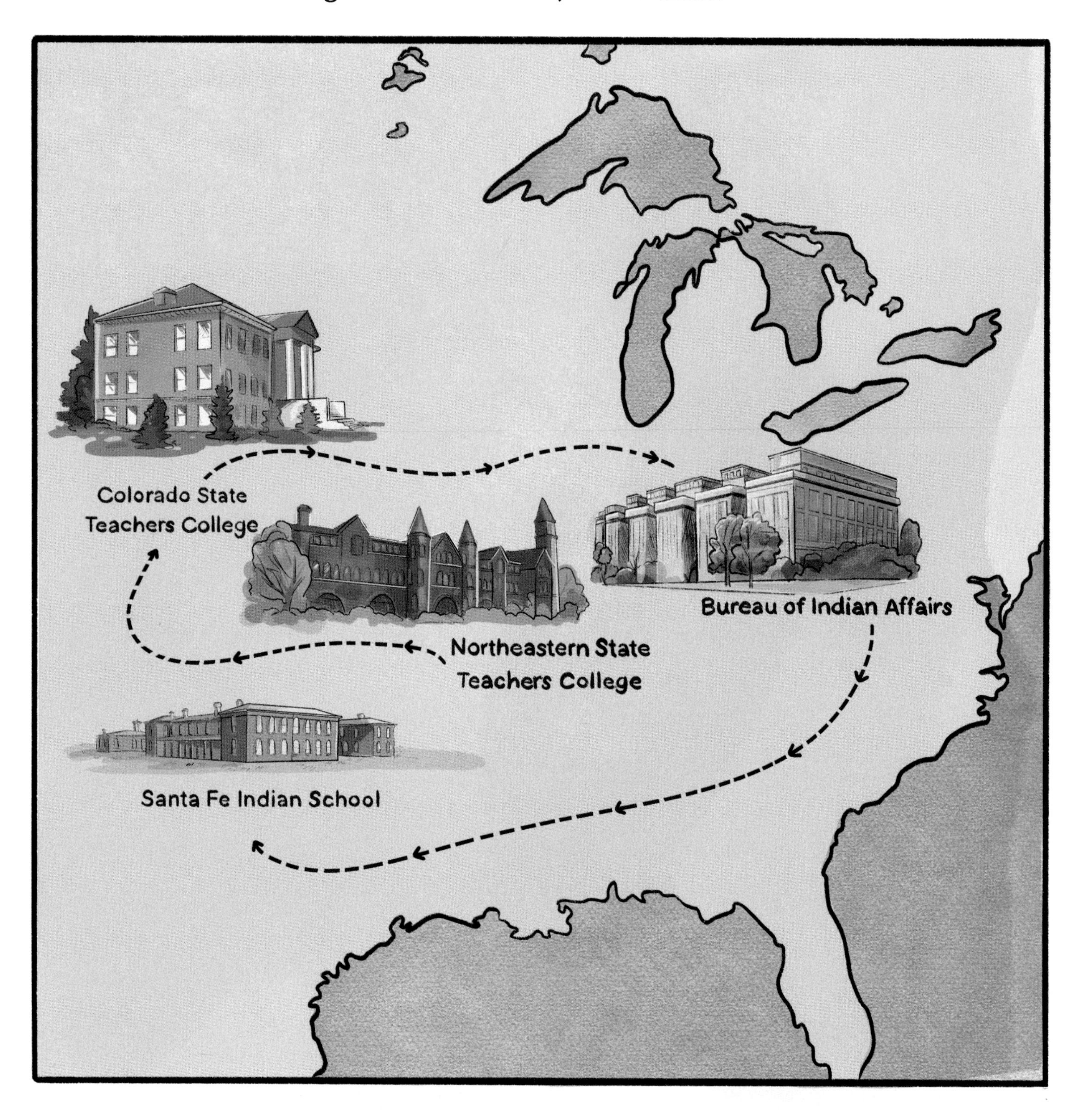

The Cherokee value of instructing in a gentle, thoughtful way guided Mary as she encouraged the next generation of Pueblo and Navajo girls to learn and excel.

Mary soon found that others outside the classroom needed her math and science knowledge too.

After the United States entered World War II in 1941, Mary left her teaching career and moved once again, this time to Los Angeles, California. Mary got a job as a mathematician for the Lockheed Aircraft Corporation. She helped solve a design problem affecting the safe operation of the P-38 Lightning fighter, one of Lockheed's fast-flying planes, and she enjoyed the research.

Now she wanted to design and build aircraft and spacecraft as an engineer.

At that time, only men served as engineers in the large corporation. Mary thought back to when she was the lone girl in her math and science classes. She wasn't intimidated.

But she knew she needed more training.

Mary focused. The company helped her take engineering classes at a nearby university. She had to balance her job duties and homework.

Would the men Mary worked with accept her as their equal?

They did! Mary became Lockheed's first female engineer and helped other women join the field.

She modeled the Cherokee value of working together in mind and heart. She shared her knowledge and asked questions to improve designs. Her male colleagues respected her intellect, her drive to solve problems, and how she worked in the team.

None of them realized, though, what would come next.

With World War II almost over, the race between the United States and the Soviet Union to reach outer space sped up. The company selected Mary to be one of forty engineers in a supersecret work team. Mary described their mission as "taking the theoretical and making it real."

What did that even mean?

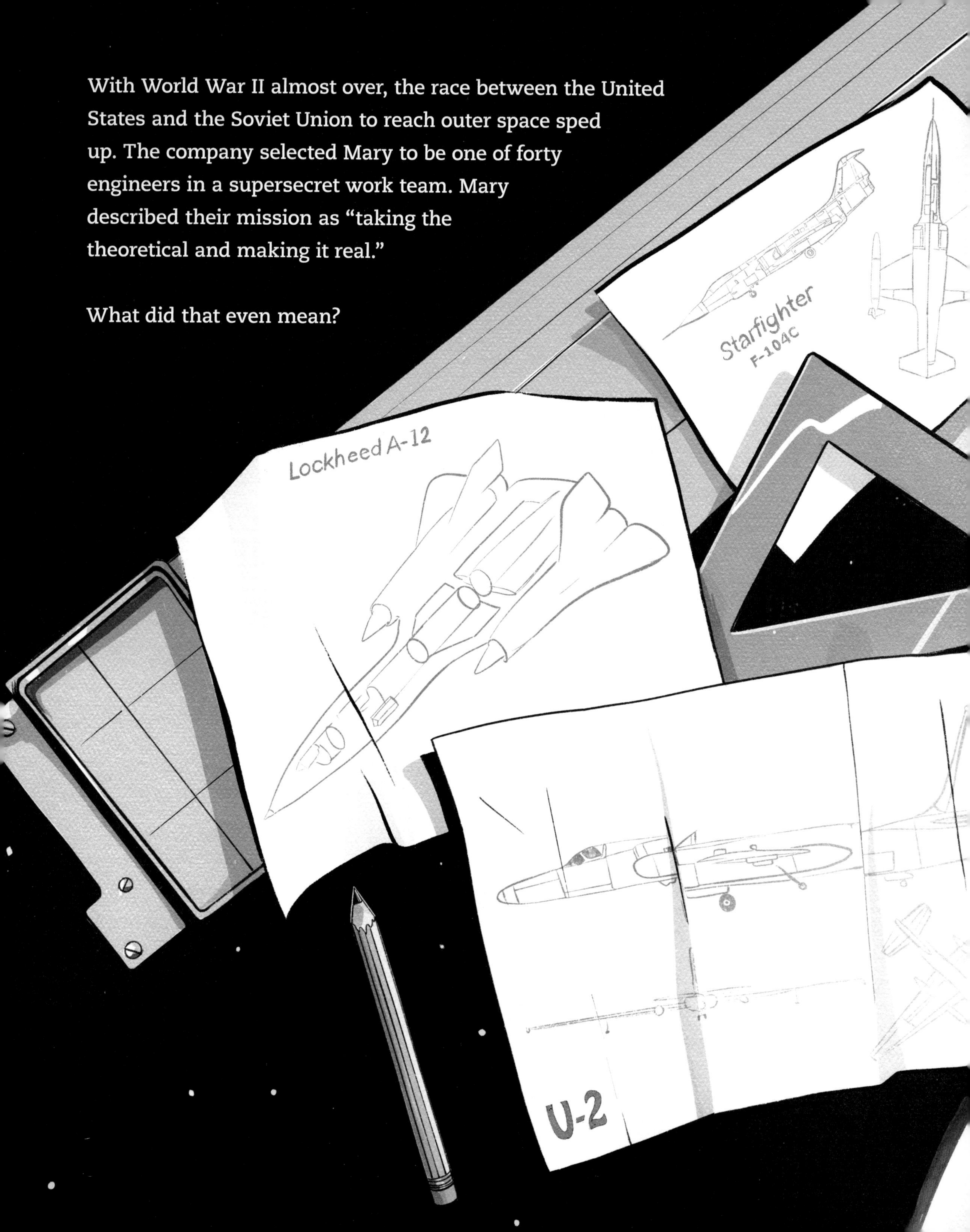

It meant Mary worked on projects that people had only imagined and some no one had ever thought of before. No vessel had ever flown nonstop around Earth—with or without a pilot. Flying *beyond* Earth? That seemed impossible!

Determined, she and her colleagues would figure out how to do it.

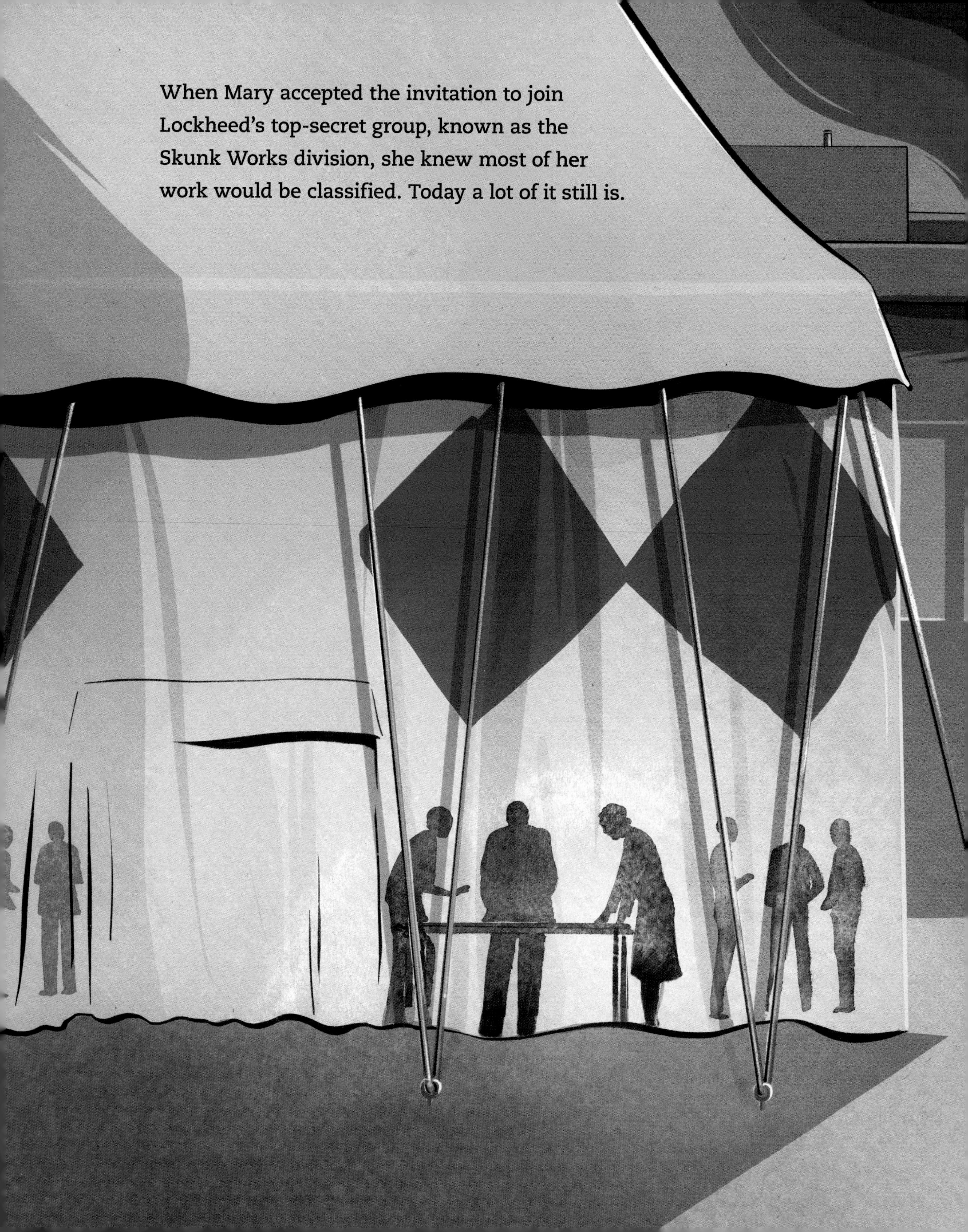

When Mary accepted the invitation to join Lockheed's top-secret group, known as the Skunk Works division, she knew most of her work would be classified. Today a lot of it still is.

When Mary appeared on a "guess my job" TV game show, she surprised the host when her line of work was finally revealed.

Even though Mary worked on world-changing projects, she never sought the spotlight.

Along with her colleagues, Mary researched orbiting satellites—like those that monitor weather patterns and send signals to televisions. She designed concepts for space travel to Venus and Mars. Her critical work on spacecraft later helped the Apollo space program send astronauts to the moon!

But what if nobody ever knew her name or recognized her as the important engineer she was?

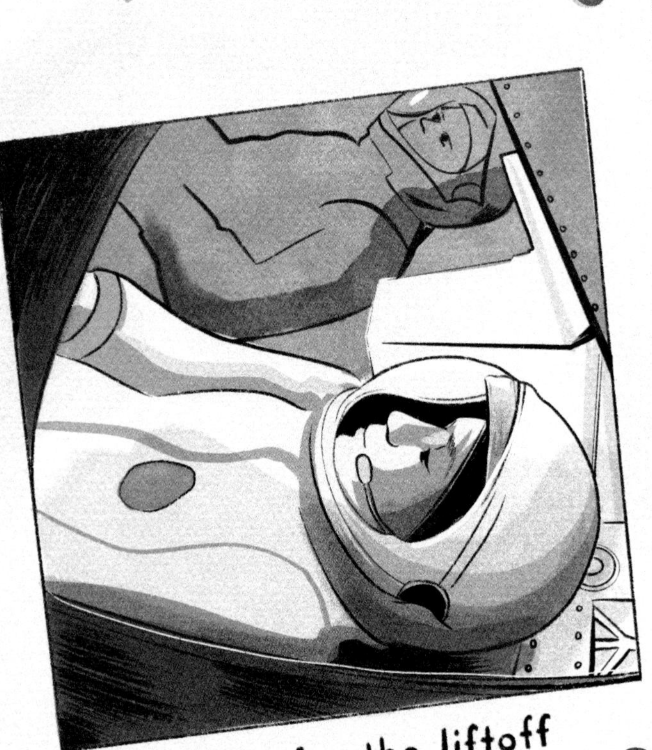

Braced for the liftoff

Millions living better thanks to moonwalk

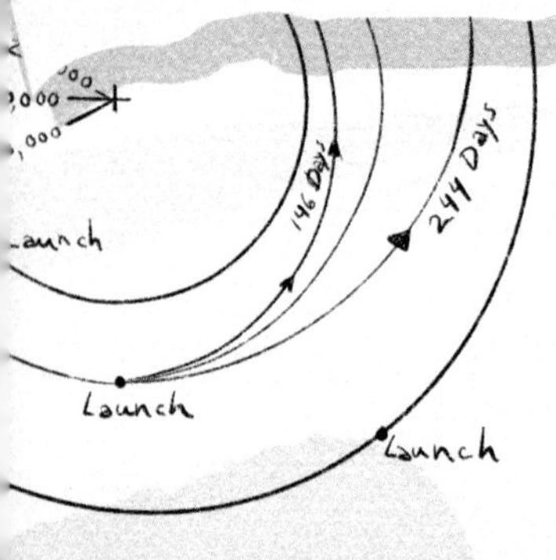

Gemini called first true flying machine in space
LAUNCH
ORBIT 3
ORBIT 2
ORBIT 1
Primary Planned Landing
Suited up for space
Walking 100 miles above Ear

RAFT DESIGN
ketch Book
AIRCRAFT
LOCKHEED AIRCRAFT CORP
Prepared
Checked
Approved
Model
VELOCITY
ANGLE

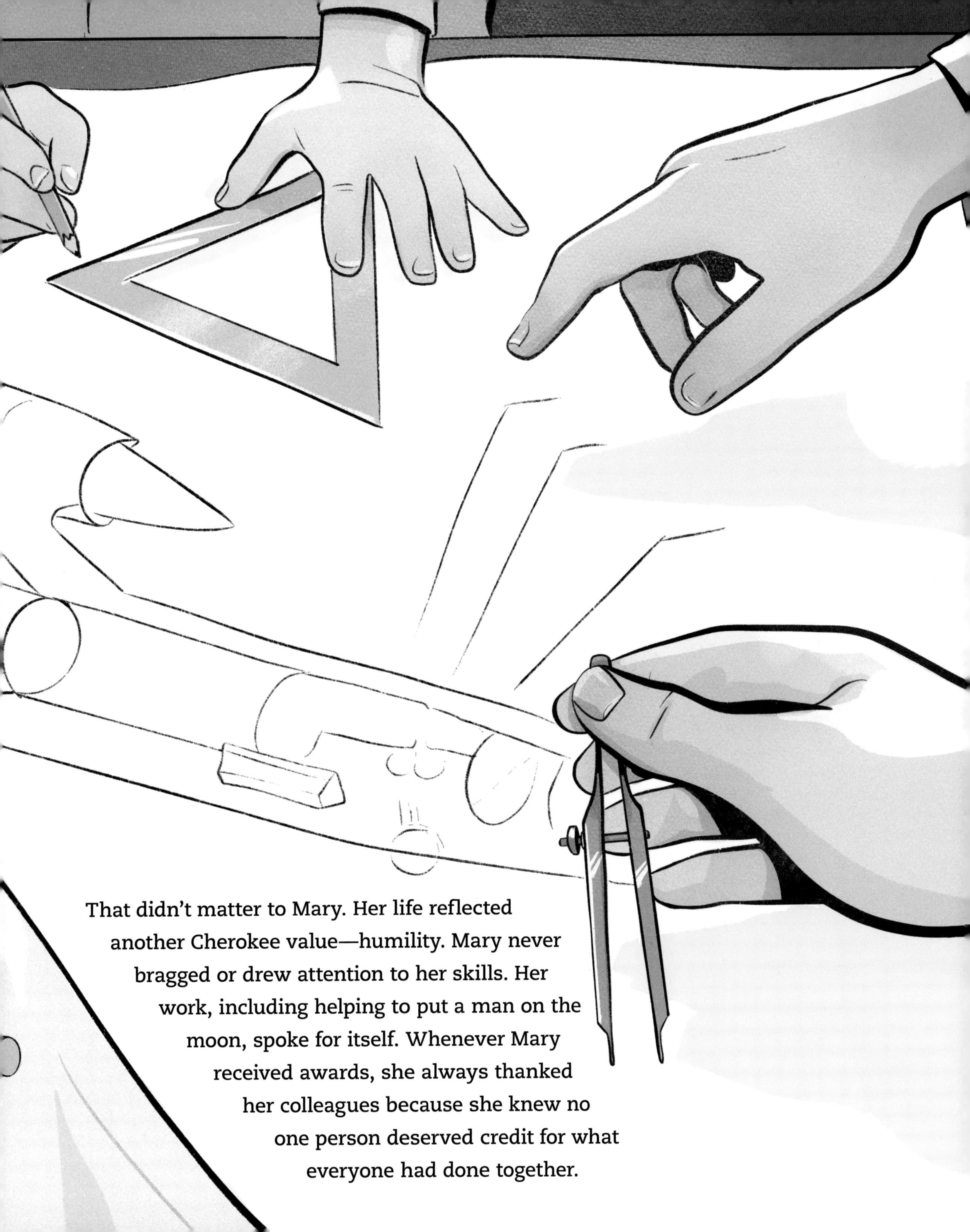

That didn't matter to Mary. Her life reflected another Cherokee value—humility. Mary never bragged or drew attention to her skills. Her work, including helping to put a man on the moon, spoke for itself. Whenever Mary received awards, she always thanked her colleagues because she knew no one person deserved credit for what everyone had done together.

In her quiet, steadfast way, Mary kept right on blazing a trail for others to follow for the rest of her life.

Although her work was classified, Mary still had much to share. She never stopped recruiting American Indians and young women to study math and science and helping support them to become engineers.

Mary's work and her legacy of service have helped many others become trailblazers too.

TIMELINE

AUGUST 9, 1908: Mary Golda Ross (known as Gold to her family) is born in Park Hill, Oklahoma, to Cherokee Nation citizens William Wallace Ross Jr. and Mary Henrietta (Moore) Ross. She is the second of their five children.

MAY 18, 1925: Graduates from high school at the age of sixteen.

JULY 19, 1928: Graduates from college at the age of twenty.

1927–1935: Begins teaching while still in college and continues for nearly a decade. She teaches math and science in rural public high schools in White Oak (1927–1928), Osage (1928–1930, also principal 1929–1930), and Barnsdall, Oklahoma (1930–1935).

1932–1934 & 1937–1938: Takes graduate courses at Colorado State Teachers College (now the University of Northern Colorado at Greeley) in the summers, including every astronomy class offered there.

1935–1937: Briefly works as a statistical clerk at the Bureau of Indian Affairs (BIA) in Washington, DC.

1937–1942: The BIA's Education Department sends her to New Mexico to advise female students at their boarding school. Earns a master's degree in math from Colorado State Teachers College in August 1938.

JULY 7, 1942: After visiting friends in Los Angeles and encouraged by her father, applies and is hired by the large Lockheed Aircraft Corporation as a mathematical research assistant. The United States had entered World War II the previous year, and there was a shortage of skilled workers with her mathematical background. She assists engineers to correct a design problem with the P-38 Lightning fighter plane that had caused the death of a test pilot and other pilots in combat.

1949: Receives her certification in mechanical engineering from the University of California at Los Angeles. Also studies aeronautics and missile and celestial mechanics at UCLA through 1952.

1950: Officially becomes Lockheed's first woman engineer.

1953: Selected to serve as one of forty engineers, and the only woman, in Lockheed's top-secret Skunk Works group. With no room inside Lockheed's buildings, the group worked in a rented circus tent next to a smelly manufacturing plant. Their name and later registered trademark derived from that.

1953: Cofounds and serves as a charter member of the Los Angeles section of the Society of Women Engineers. She serves the organization on a national level for decades, working to make the engineering field more inclusive.

1957: Classified work is propelled forward when the Soviet Union launches Sputnik, the world's first satellite. The United States does not want to fall behind in the space race and rushes to catch up.

A portrait of Mary Golda Ross from the mid-1900s

1958: She appears on *What's My Line?*—a TV show in which celebrities guess the guest's occupation. The studio and home-viewing audience see Mary's job listed as "Designs Rocket Missiles and Satellites (Lockheed Aircraft)" on the screen.

JULY 20, 1969: Describes that she felt a quiet pride knowing "a Cherokee woman from Park Hill, Oklahoma, helped put a man on the moon" when astronaut Neil Armstrong makes history as the first human to walk on the moon's surface.

1970: Coauthors NASA's Planetary Flight Handbook Volume 3 about space travel to Mars and Venus.

AUGUST 31, 1973: Retires from Lockheed as a Senior Advanced Systems Staff Engineer.

1973: The Santa Clara Valley section of the Society of Women Engineers establishes a scholarship in her name. Continues her work to open up more channels for women and American Indians to enter the fields of math and engineering.

1984: Receives an honorary life membership from the American Indian Science and Engineering Society.

1985: Is awarded the Council of Energy Resource Tribes' Achievement Award, which is then renamed as the Mary G. Ross Award for future recipients.

1992: Is inducted into the Silicon Valley Engineering Council Hall of Fame, only the second woman to receive that honor. A scholarship is established in her name by the Society of Women Engineers.

1993: Is awarded the University of Northern Colorado Alumni Association's Trailblazer Award.

1994: Is named Outstanding Alumnus by Northeastern State University's Alumni Association.

SEPTEMBER 21, 2004: At the age of ninety-six, she attends the launch of the National Museum of the American Indian (NMAI) in Washington, DC. She participates in the Native Nations Procession and attends NMAI's Opening Ceremony on the National Mall.

Mary (*left*) presents Akiko Inoue with a certificate from the Society of Women Engineers in 1993.

APRIL 29, 2008: Dies in Los Altos, California, just three months shy of her one-hundredth birthday.

AUGUST 9, 2018: Is commemorated by Google with a Google Doodle on what would've been her 110th birthday.

2019: Is selected as an honoree of a design for a United States Native American dollar coin with the theme "American Indians in the Space Program."

AUTHOR'S NOTE

As a child, I loved reading biographies from my school library. Slim volumes shared the lives, important work, and struggles of men and women—nearly all of them white. Yet I knew the Cherokee Nation had many citizens serving others and succeeding in their professions. But their stories remained untold.

Mary Golda Ross is one of those Cherokee citizens, remaining true to her tribal upbringing while contributing her intellect and skills to the greater world. To write this story, I visited with her cousin, Bruce Ross, who shared that I should visit the archives at her alma mater Northeastern State University to complement the research I had already done. Being able to hold Mary's slide rule, read through notebooks she'd filled with equations, and thumb through books she referenced as she worked gave me an even greater appreciation of Mary's vision, research, and work ethic. Her story deserves to be shared.

Along with Mary Golda Ross, my mother and I participated in the Native Nations Procession at the National Museum of the American Indian's opening day in 2004. I only wish I had known she was one of the elders there within our large Cherokee Nation delegation. I regret not being able to visit with her in person that day and thank her for being a trailblazer for so many.

Mary drew on her status as the first known Native American female engineer to make sure those coming after her would be welcome in math and engineering. She strongly supported the American Indian Science and Engineering Society with vocal and financial backing. Mary gave talks to high school and college students encouraging young women and Native Americans to get a firm foundation in math and train for technical careers.

She lived the Cherokee values she had been raised with, benefiting us all in doing so.

FOUR CHEROKEE VALUES

SYLLABARY: ᎾᏂᏏᎾᏒ ᎤᏁᏉᏤᎲ ᏂᎦᎥ ᎢᎬᎾᏕᎾ Ꮎ ᎬᏅᎢ
TRANSLITERATION: nanisinasv unequotsehv nigav igvnadena na gvnvi
PRONUNCIATION: nah-NEE-see-NAH-suh oo-neh-KWOH-jay-huh nee-gah-uh ee-guh-nah-DAY-nah nah guh-NUH-ee
ENGLISH: gaining skills in all areas of life

SYLLABARY: ᏓᎾᎵᏍᏕᎵᏍᎬ ᏚᏂᎸᏫᏍᏓᏁᎲ ᎠᏂᏐᎢ ᎬᏗ
TRANSLITERATION: danalisdelisgv dunilvwisdanehv anisoi gvdi
PRONUNCIATION: dah-nah-LEEs-day-LEEs-guh duh-nee-LUH-wees-duh-NEH-huh ah-nee-SO-ee GUH-dee
ENGLISH: working cooperatively with others

SYLLABARY: ᎤᎾᎵᏃᎯᏴ ᏄᏢᏉᏛᎾ ᎾᏳᏃ ᎠᏂᏐᎢ ᎨᏦᎵᏤᎲ ᏣᎦᏙᎲᏒᎯ ᎨᏒᎢ
TRANSLITERATION: unalinohiyv nutlvquodvna nayuno anisoi getsolitsehv tsagadohvsvhi gesvi
PRONUNCIATION: oo-nah-ah-LEE-no-hee-yuh new-tluh-kwuo-DUH-nah nah-you-no ah-nee-SO-ee gay-jo-LEE-jay-huh jah-gah-doe-huh-SUH-hee gay-SUH-ee
ENGLISH: remaining humble when others recognize your talents

SYLLABARY: ᎠᏍᏕᎵᏍᎩ ᏳᎵᏍᏙᏗ ᎢᎦᏘᎭ ᏗᏕᎶᏆᏍᏗ ᎠᎴ ᎤᎾᏜᏅᏓᏕᎲ ᎾᏍᎩᎾ ᎯᎦᏓ
TRANSLITERATION: asdelisgi yulisdodi igatiha dideloquasdi ale unadlanvdadehv nasgina higada
PRONUNCIATION: ahs-day-LEEs-jee you-lees-DO-dee ee-gah-tee-HA dee-DAY-low-KWAHS-dee ah-LAY oo-nah-dlah-nuh-dah-DAY-huh nahs-GEE-nah hee-GAH-dah
ENGLISH: helping ensure equal education and opportunity for all

SOURCE NOTES

"*Do your best . . . Indian heritage*": Will Chavez, "Mary Ross Used Knowledge of Mathematics to Become Successful Engineer," *Cherokee Phoenix*, May 2008, B7.

"*The world is . . . farther and faster*": Cherokee Nation, "The Cherokee Nation Remembers Mary Golda Ross, the First Woman Engineer for Lockheed," news release, May 13, 2008, https://cherokee.org/News/Stories/Archive_2008/23649.

"*Taking the theoretical . . . real*": Brad Agnew, "Cherokee Engineer a Space Exploration Pioneer," Tahlequah (OK) Daily Press, March 27, 2016, https://www.tahlequahdailypress.com/news/features/cherokee-engineer-a-space-exploration-pioneer/article_bd715fba-f395-11e5-b144-4b85a6dec5bb.html#:~:text=What%20shaped%20their%20decision%20has,in%20the%20exploration%20of%20space.

"*A Cherokee woman . . . on the moon*": Agnew.

Back cover: Weimers, Leigh. "The Sky Was the Limit for This Teacher From Cherokee County." *San Jose Mercury News*. October 30, 1994.

BIBLIOGRAPHY

Agnew, Brad. "Cherokee Engineer a Space Exploration Pioneer." *Tahlequah (OK) Daily Press*, March 27, 2016. https://www.tahlequahdailypress.com/news/features/cherokee-engineer-a-space-exploration-pioneer/article_bd715fba-f395-11e5-b144-4b85a6dec5bb.html#:~:text=What%20shaped%20their%20decision%20has,in%20the%20exploration%20of%20space.

———. "'Golda' Ross Left Teaching to Support War Effort." *Tahlequah (OK) Daily Press*, March 20, 2016. https://www.tahlequahdailypress.com/news/golda-ross-left-teaching-to-support-war-effort/article_c500cbc4-eeba-11e5-9b57-2b127651fcb5.html.

Blakemore, Erin. "This Little-Known Math Genius Helped America Reach the Stars." *Smithsonian Magazine*, March 29, 2017. https://www.smithsonianmag.com/smithsonian-institution/little-known-math-genius-helped-america-reach-stars-180962700/.

Chavez, Will. "Mary Ross Used Knowledge of Mathematics to Become Successful Engineer." *Cherokee Phoenix*, May 2008, B7.

Cherokee Nation. "The Cherokee Nation Remembers Mary Golda Ross, the First Woman Engineer for Lockheed." News release, May 13, 2008. https://cherokee.org/News/Stories/Archive_2008/23649.

"Game 1: Miss Mary G. Ross—'Designs Rocket Missiles and Satellites (Lockheed Aircraft).'" *What's My Line*, episode 420, June 22, 1958. YouTube video, 26:03. https://www.youtube.com/watch?v=vFlvpMf-dIo.

Holmes, Meredith. "What We Really Did after the War." *SWE: Magazine of the Society of Women Engineers*, Spring 2014, 20–27. https://drive.google.com/file/d/1BA_BNK0nI8UXj37Y8RuI2IGYYhh-wdBz/view.

Judkins, Maggie. "CCAC Selects Native American Dollar Designs." *Numismatic News*, June 23, 2017. http://www.numismaticnews.net/article/ccac-selects-native-american-dollar-designs.

"Mary G. Ross' 110th Birthday." Google.com, August 9, 2018. https://www.google.com/doodles/mary-g-ross-110th-birthday.

Sheppard, Laurel M. "An Interview with Mary Ross: First American Indian Women Engineer, Aerospace Pioneer Returns to Her Native American Roots." Lash Publications. Accessed July 4, 2018. http://www.nn.net/lash/maryross.htm.

"Skunk Works® Origin Story." Lockheed Martin. Accessed June 26, 2020. https://www.lockheedmartin.com/en-us/who-we-are/business-areas/aeronautics/skunkworks/skunk-works-origin-story.html.

For future engineers, mathematicians, and scientists, "do the best you can" as Mary would say. I'm rooting for you.
—T.S.

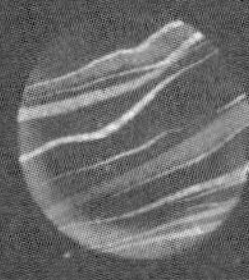

For Mrs. Barbara Sunday and all the teachers at Sentinel Secondary who encouraged me to follow an unusual path—with gratitude
—N.D.

Acknowledgments
This book would not have been possible without: Bruce Ross and the archives staff at Northeastern State University—Brenda Kaye Bradford, director, and Blain McLain, special assistant—for helping me access critical primary sources about Mary's life and career; aerospace engineer Dr. Joseph Connolly, mechanical engineer Dr. Powtawche Valerino, and wind tunnel manager Richard F. Bozak at NASA for their review of the technical information shared in the art; and John Ross and Wade Blevins for their assistance with the Cherokee language featured.

Millbrook Press™
An imprint of Lerner Publishing Group, Inc.
241 First Avenue North
Minneapolis, MN 55401 USA

For reading levels and more information, look up this title at www.lernerbooks.com.

Image credits: Pictures From History/Newscom, p. 28; Walter P. Reuther Library, Wayne State University, p. 29.

Designed by Danielle Carnito.
Main body text set in Caecilia Com 75 Bold. Typeface provided by Linotype AG.
The illustrations in this book were created with pencil, ink, and Procreate.

Library of Congress Cataloging-in-Publication Data

Names: Sorell, Traci, author. | Donovan, Natasha, illustrator.
Title: Classified : the secret career of Mary Golda Ross, Cherokee aerospace engineer / Traci Sorell ; illustrated by Natasha Donovan.
Description: Minneapolis : Millbrook Press, [2021] | Includes bibliographical references. | Audience: Ages 7–11 | Audience: Grades 2–3 | Summary: "Mary Golda Ross designed classified projects for Lockheed Aircraft Corporation as the company's first female engineer. Find out how her passion for math and the Cherokee values she was raised with shaped her life and work"— Provided by publisher.
Identifiers: LCCN 2020021725 (print) | LCCN 2020021726 (ebook) | ISBN 9781541579149 (trade hardcover) | ISBN 9781728419015 (ebook)
Subjects: LCSH: Ross, Mary Golda—Juvenile literature. | Women aerospace engineers—United States—Biography—Juvenile literature. | Cherokee Indians—United States—Biography—Juvenile literature.
Classification: LCC TL540.R655 S67 2021 (print) | LCC TL540.R655 (ebook) | DDC 629.1092 [B]—dc23

LC record available at https://lccn.loc.gov/2020021725
LC ebook record available at https://lccn.loc.gov/2020021726

Manufactured in the United States of America
1-47183-47900-7/2/2020